# Dedicated to

# Gianna

# My Inspiration

*AuthorHouse™*
*1663 Liberty Drive*
*Bloomington, IN 47403*
*www.authorhouse.com*
*Phone: 833-262-8899*

*Because of the dynamic nature of the Internet, any web addresses or links contained in this book may have changed since publication and may no longer be valid. The views expressed in this work are solely those of the author and do not necessarily reflect the views of the publisher, and the publisher hereby disclaims any responsibility for them.*

*This book is printed on acid-free paper.*

*ISBN: 978-1-6655-5444-2 (sc)*
*ISBN: 978-1-6655-5446-6 (hc)*
*ISBN: 978-1-6655-5445-9 (e)*

*Print information available on the last page.*

*Published by AuthorHouse  03/17/2022*

**author**HOUSE®

# MONARCH LIFE

## "Metamorphosis"

### Gerri Endean

# The story of a Monarch Butterfly on Maui!

First, the lady Monarch lays her eggs
on the leaves of a milkweed plant.

Do you see the tiny white egg?

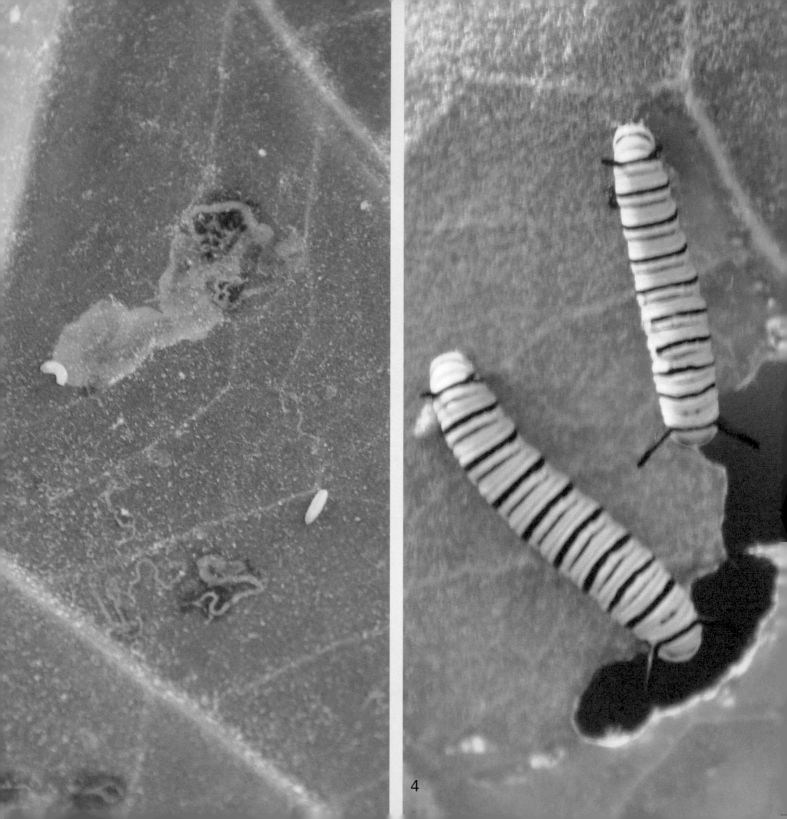

4

## Caterpillar Stage

Caterpillars live for 10–14 days.

Every couple days they get too big for their skin and have to shed it.

This is called "molting". Look for the black patch of skin. It is sort of like when you grow too big for your clothes!

Lots of
company!

When the caterpillar is ready to become a butterfly it attaches to the leaf and forms this "J".

It sheds its skin one more time, and takes a nap for 10–14 days. This is called the Chrysalis stage.

While in this stage the magic of turning into a Monarch Butterfly is taking place. You can almost see the butterfly as it grows. Do you see it?

Sometimes we have to rescue a chrysalis that has fallen off the milkweed and put them in a nursery!

This is the beginning of the birth of a new butterfly! Can you see the leg?

The new butterfly emerges from the chrysalis. See how tiny it is!

The wings are very small, and the belly is very big! Fluid from the belly is pumped into the wings to make them grow!

Can you see the changes in the wings as they grow bigger and bigger?

This takes about 3 hours. As they grow, they dry. Pretty soon our Monarch is ready to fly away!

# FUN FACTS ABOUT MONARCH BUTTERFLIES

1. Butterflies taste with their feet!
2. Males have a black dot on each hind wing.
3. They drink nectar through a straw-like "mouth".
4. Butterflies fly at about 5-6 miles per hour.
5. Monarchs are attracted to Orange, Yellow, Red, Pink and Purple flowers.

Printed in the United States
by Baker & Taylor Publisher Services